Wunderlust

The Photos of a Traveling Muse

Photos by Michael Thaxton

All Photos Owned and Copyrighted by

Michael Thaxton Photography

Wunderlust – a strong desire to travel.

I have been traveling since I was 17 and joined the Navy. Today, I can say there is a lot of travelling left to do in my life. I am satisfied with the journeys I have taken so far.

This book is a snapshot of just a few years of being in Upstate New York and St. Louis, Missouri. I had to sort through thousands of photos to choose these fifty.

I would like to thank a few people for encouraging me and helping get this book completed:

George Mills – the basic skills you taught me in High School helped create the images in this book.

My Mother – Barbara Strozyk Gravelle – Love you, you have always been an encouragement to me. I had to release this book on your 70th birthday to pay tribute to you for giving me my first camera.

Pastor Tamara Franchuk – words can't thank you enough for the encouraging words and prayers.

My children and grandchildren – you guys are the driving force behind all this creativity.

And last – **Sheree (S. Coop)** – I love you, you have pushed me to the limits and this book would not be possible without you.

To see more of my photograhy check out my facebook page

www.facebook.com/michaelthaxtonphotos

All these prints are available for sale, feel free to contact me at mthaxton@gmail.com.

The Garage
St Louis, Mo
Spring 2016

Abandoned House
Churchville, NY
Summer 2016

Rock Dam

Corbett's Glenn, Penfield, NY
Summer 2016

Wave Crash
Summerville Pier, Rochester, NY
Summer 2016

Water Under The Bridge
Rochester, NY
Summer 2016

South Wedge
Rochester, NY
Summer 2016

Sunset on Lake Ontario

Summer 2014

The Bridge
Rochester, NY
Summer 2016

Light At The End Of The Tunnel
Rochester, NY
Summer 2016

The Column
Rochester, NY
Summer 2016

Volleyball Courts
Charlotte Beach, Rochester, NY
Summer 2016

Port of Rochester

Rochester, NY
Summer 2016

Landlocked
Rochester, NY
Summer 2016

Middle Falls
Genesee River
Rochester, NY
Summer 2016

Dry Bones

Memorial Art Gallery
Rochester, NY
Summer 2016

Sunlight

St. Joseph's Park
Rochester, NY
Fall 2014

Flowers in Charlotte
Rochester, NY
Summer 2016

Open Tracks
Rochester, NY
Summer 2016

Webster Park

Webster, NY
Summer 2016

Reflection Pool
Missouri Botanical Gardens
St Louis, MO
Spring 2016

Tree of Life

Missouri Botanical Gardens
St Louis, MO
Spring 2016

Gateway Arch
St Louis, MO
Spring 2016

Iron Sharpens Iron
"Steel Revisited"
St Louis, MO
Spring 2016

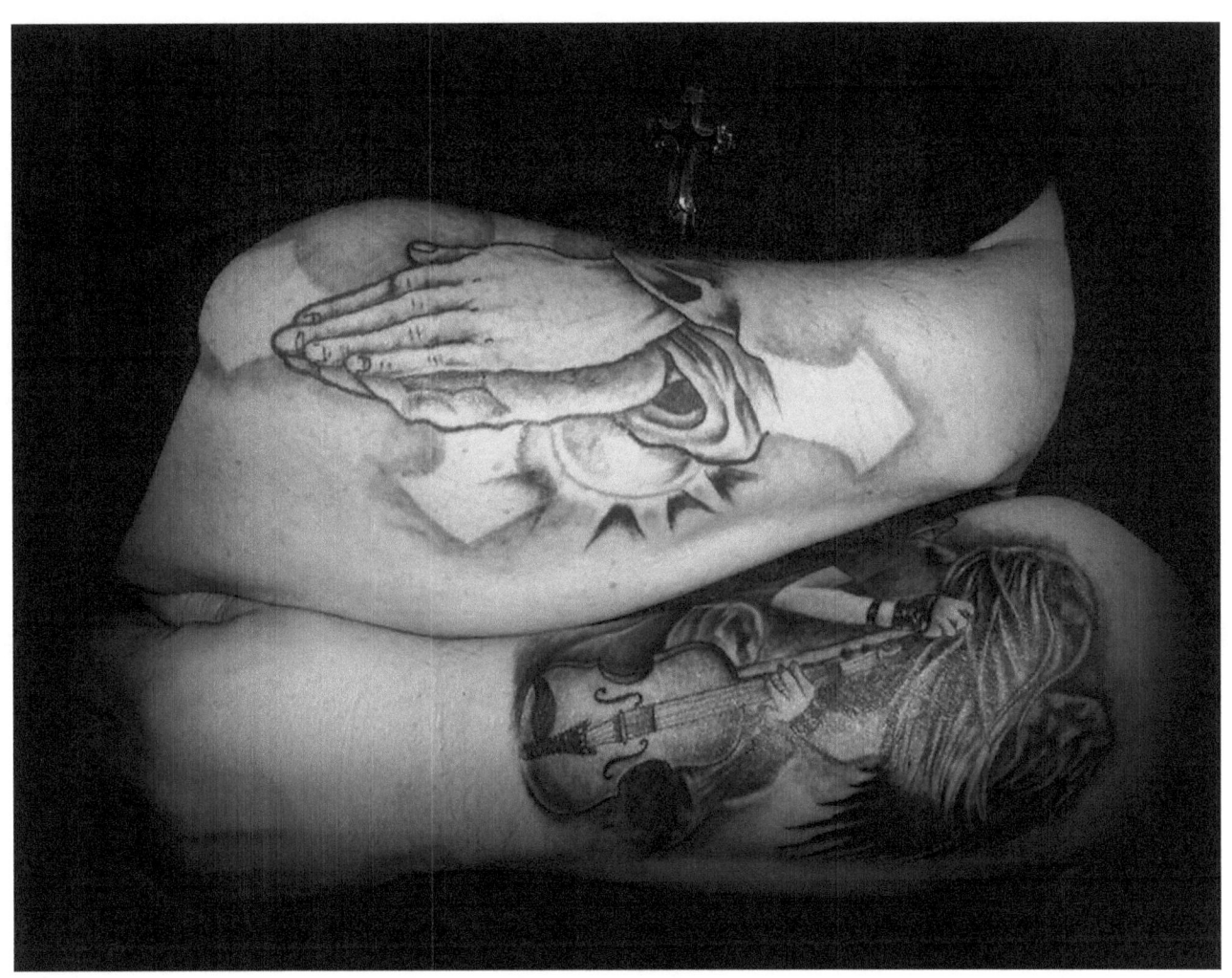

My Ink
Rochester, NY
Fall 2013

After the Storm
Crescent Beach Hotel
Greece, NY
Winter 2016

In The Morning
Maplewood Park and Rose Garden
Rochester, NY
Summer 2012

Heroes
Jefferson Barracks National Military Cemetery
St Louis, MO
Spring 2016

Unknown U.S. Soldier
Jefferson Barracks National Military Cemetery
St Louis, MO
Spring 2016

Grace Church
Maryland Heights, MO
Spring 2016

Chain of Rocks Bridge Rest Area
St Louis, MO
Spring 2016

Phillips 66
Chain of Rocks Bridge
St Louis, MO
Spring 2016

Chain of Rocks Bridge

St Louis, MO
Spring 2016

Route 66 Bench
Chain of Rocks Bridge
St Louis, MO
Spring 2016

Missouri Route 66
Chain of Rocks Bridge
St Louis, MO
Spring 2016

Charlotte Pier at Sunset

Rochester, NY
Summer 2016

The Pier at Sunset
Charlotte Pier, Rochester, NY
Summer 2016

Sunset Cruise
Genesee River, Rochester, NY
Summer 2016

Webster Park Pier

Webster, NY
Spring 2016

Irondequoit Bay Pier
Irondequoit, NY
Summer 2016

Silo
Churchville, NY
Spring 2016

The Walk of Life
Missouri Botanical Gardens
St Louis, MO
Spring 2016

Sailboat

Lake Ontario, NY
Summer 2014

Charlotte Lighthouse
Rochester, NY
Summer 2016

Casters
St Louis, MO
Spring 2016

Walking the Pier
Webster, NY
Spring 2016

Abandoned
St Louis, MO
Spring 2016

Driftwood
Summerville Beach
Rochester, NY
Summer 2015

The Guardian
Genesee River
Rochester, NY
Spring 2015

Coast Guard Station
Rochester, NY
Fall 2013

Wedding Reception
The Barn
Rush, NY
Summer 2015